The Opposite Cousins

by Barbara A. Donovan
illustrated by Holli Conger

Scott Foresman
is an imprint of

Glenview, Illinois • Boston, Massachusetts • Mesa, Arizona
Shoreview, Minnesota • Upper Saddle River, New Jersey

Illustrator Holli Conger

Photographs
Every effort has been made to secure permission and provide appropriate credit for photographic material. The publisher deeply regrets any omission and pledges to correct errors called to its attention in subsequent editions.

Unless otherwise acknowledged, all photographs are the property of Pearson Education, Inc.

Photo locators denoted as follows: Top (T), Center (C), Bottom (B), Left (L), Right (R), Background (Bkgd)

12 (T) Reinhard Dirscherl/Bruce Coleman Inc.; (C) blickwinkel/Alamy Images; (B) Masa Ushioda/V&W/Bruce Coleman Inc.

ISBN 13: 978-0-328-39406-7
ISBN 10: 0-328-39406-8

8 9 10 VOFL 16 15 14 13

Samantha smiled. Her cousin Jeff would be here soon. Their week at the lake would be perfect.

Samantha had a vision of teaching her cousin how to fish. They could fish every day! What could be better?

"They're here!" shouted Samantha. She ran to greet Jeff and Uncle Henry.

But Jeff raced for the cabin as quick as a bat.

"Don't mind Jeff," said Uncle Henry. "The battery for his computer died. Jeff is eager to plug it in."

Each day Samantha hiked with Mom and Dad. She swam in the lake. She fished.

Jeff stayed inside and played on his computer.

At one time, Samantha and Jeff liked the same things. Now they were opposites.

It rained on the third day.

Jeff asked, "Would you like to play a computer game with me?"

The two cousins played together all day. They had a lot of fun.

The next day Samantha asked Jeff to go fishing.

"Maybe later," Jeff said.

Once again, Samantha fished alone. Jeff stayed inside.

That night a storm blew in. CRACK! Lightning split the sky. Thunder boomed. The power went out. Luckily there was wood to use as fuel for the fireplace.

The next morning Jeff yelled, "Oh, no!"

The storm had ruined his computer. It was dead for the rest of his term at the lake.

Samantha offered to teach Jeff how to fish.
"Why not?" Jeff said.

Before long Jeff shouted, "I've got a bite!" Jeff caught his first fish. It was a brown trout.

The cousins fished every day after that. They even planned a fishing game for the computer.

Then it was time for Jeff and Uncle Henry to go home. "I'll call you about our fishing game!" Jeff called out.

"I can't wait!" Samantha called back.

Opposites can have fun after all.

Freshwater Fish

Freshwater fish live in lakes, ponds, rivers, and streams. Fish need food and oxygen in the water to live. Here are three common freshwater fish.

Brown trout live in lakes and streams. Their bodies are brownish with many red or orange spots. Young brown trout eat insects. Adults eat other fish.

Common carp can live just about anywhere. They like clear water. Muddy water is fine, too. This fish will eat almost any bait.

White catfish live in ponds, lakes, and rivers. They have feelers on their chins. These feelers help them find food.